Photo credit: Magdalena Bors

Angela Costi is also known as Αγγελική Κωστή among the Cypriot-Greek diaspora. In Cyprus, her maternal grandmother utilised her embroidery skills to try to rise above poverty, creating the renowned *Lefkarathika* embroidery of Cyprus. In 1958, her parents left Cyprus to escape poverty, civil unrest and imminent war.

Travel and migration have been part of Costi's writing history. In 1995, she received a travel award from the Australian National Languages and Literacy Board to study Ancient Greek Drama in Greece. In 2009, she travelled to Japan with funding from the Australia Council for the Arts to work on an international collaboration involving her poetry and Japan-based, Stringraphy Ensemble. Since 1994, her poetry, stories, essays and reviews have been widely published nationally and internationally.

She is a graduate of both Law (Melbourne University) and Professional Writing and Editing (RMIT University), and this has enabled her to practice as a lawyer and community artist. She has worked for many years in the social justice sector.

Other works by Angela Costi

Poetry
Dinted Halos (2003)
Prayers for the Wicked (2005)
Honey & Salt (2007)
Lost in Mid-Verse (2014)

Plays and Performance-texts
The Sound of Incense (1994)
Panayiota (1997)
Welcome Matt (1999)
Un-Beat-Able (2000)
Divine Law (2000)
Shimmer (2001)
Signatures (2002)
Relocated (2003)
A Nest of Cinnamon (2009)

Co-authored with Angela Bailey
Relocated – a tribute to tenants, Kensington Public Housing Estate (2003)

Video poems
Making Lace (2020)
Shelter (2020)
The Routine of Space (2020)
Kinaesthetic Grace (2020)

An Embroidery of Old Maps and New

Angela Costi

First published by Spinifex Press, 2021

Spinifex Press Pty Ltd
PO Box 5270, North Geelong, VIC 3215, Australia
PO Box 105, Mission Beach, QLD 4852, Australia

women@spinifexpress.com.au
www.spinifexpress.com.au

Copyright © Angela Costi, 2021

The moral right of the author has been asserted.

All rights reserved. Without limiting the rights under copyright reserved above, no part of this publication may be reproduced, stored in or introduced into a retrieval system, or transmitted, in any form or by any means (electronic, mechanical, photocopying, recording or otherwise) without prior written permission of both the copyright owner and the above publisher of the book.

Copying for educational purposes
Information in this book may be reproduced in whole or part for study or training purposes, subject to acknowledgement of the source and providing no commercial usage or sale of material occurs. Where copies of part or whole of the book are made under part VB of the Copyright Act, the law requires that prescribed procedures be followed. For information contact the Copyright Agency Limited.

Although experience and memory are threaded throughout, fiction supersedes this collection. Names, characters, places, services, businesses and incidents are a product of the author's imagination.

Edited by Susan Hawthorne
Cover design by Deb Snibson, MAPG
Typesetting by Helen Christie, Blue Wren Books
Typeset in Albertina
Printed and bound by CPI Group (UK) Ltd, Croydon, CR0 4YY

A catalogue record for this book is available from the National Library of Australia

ISBN: 9781925950243 (paperback)
ISBN: 9781925950250 (ebook)

This project was partially assisted by the City of Melbourne, COVID-19 Arts Grants, 2020.

To Eleni Costi
who taught me the significance of the past

Trying to leap across fields across continents
to build up a sense of complexity and density
to simulate the experience of the metropolis we don't have
to escape the parochial in a parochial environment
without denying the significant things
...
The actions of the tradition-breakers persisting in our memories
alongside the fragments of the old traditions
and now difficult to disentangle

Anna Couani, Southerly vol.55, no.3, Spring 1995

Here is a map of our country:
here is the Sea of Indifference, glazed with salt
This is the haunted river flowing from brow to groin
we dare not taste its water

Adrienne Rich, An Atlas of the Difficult World, Poems 1988–1991

Contents

From Bondi to Kyrenia	1
Arrival	2
Refugee Aerobics	3
Land Mines	4
Heavy	6
Knock Knock	8
Kostaki's Harvest Woes	10
Looping the Waves	11
Making Lace	13
Night Shift Crescendo	15
The Weed Eaters	17
The Good Citizens of Melbourne	18
Incident in Aisle 5	21
Kostaki's Signature	22
Fatigue	23
Inner Sense	24
An Extracurricular Assessment	26
The English Missionary	28
Kinaesthetic Grace	29
Coburg	31
When Coburg Lake Became a Kyrenia Wedding	32
When the Hills Hoist Became the Wishing Tree	33
Outskirts	34
The Quadrangle of Dreams	35
To Identify the Apostate	37
Goddess Nike	39
Somewhere Overseas	40
The Colour Chase	41
Shanker Hotel, New Delhi, 1991	43
'How to Drape a Saree'	44
The Summit of Choice	46
Travel with a Coward's Heart	48

Abduction	49
Calling	50
Good Night	51
Frontline	53
Yiayia is Swimming in my KeepCup	55
Australia Visits Minnesota	57
Regulation	58
The Daily Commute	59
Father	61
Homework	63
The Guest	65
Shelter	66
After Dinner	67
Diagnoses	70
Remission	71
2020	73
Ocean View	74
Abundance	75
Notes	77
Acknowledgements	81

From Bondi to Kyrenia

She watched this sea
with its loud waves
demanding the surfer
to almost fall off the board
like she did in the boat
as she stretched to catch
the last apricot
the crew member threw—
there were many hands reaching
for that taste of sunshine—
her body flung
against the boat's spine
as Poseidon opened his mouth
expecting a feed.

Arrival

You stand in front of glass,
it opens without knocking,
they have women unarmed
sitting at counters, smiling,
"Hello, how may I help you?"
They pay people to help you.

There are words you must hold like blankets in snow
'human rights'
'discrimination'.
You repeat them as third language,
they feel hot on your tongue,
they make you remember a child with broken teeth,
remember a woman with torn womb,
the man eating the dirt.
Here, you can say them
again and again
to many strangers
who will take your story
like a startled baby.
In fits and starts, you come to know words
as soldiers standing at check points
'allegation'
'evidence'.

Your story climbs their walls and waits for you
outside their office
knowing
you cannot open the hearts of words
written as law.

Refugee Aerobics

Running feet, marching hearts, waving arms,
they jump, they queue, they plunge
and squeeze into the triangle's longest line.
They are fed up with hunger
ready to barter their sinews and bones
for our fat and muscle.
They don't know the moves
yet they know how to climb onto each other's backs
to build that stack of body upon body
then get that one person at the top
to stretch beyond reach for the highest note,
hold steady when told, wait, still wait
to learn the music
before the words.

Land Mines

She tiptoed through her body,
carefully slid down the medulla
to walk like a whisper,
each step made without an explosion
brought a victor's muffled cry.
She asked her doctor, "What war did I incubate?"

Cyprus, Afghanistan, Korea, Cambodia
40,000, 55,000   each country growing people
without arms, legs, and still they continue
to gather their wood by that roadside,
go to school on the path with the new rubber foot.
El Salvador, Vietnam, Angola, Syria
continue to work, marry, have children
cook with their elbow, write with their teeth.

A schwannoma
is built to blast injury
with five trauma triggers:
activator, fuse, charge,
a power source and a body.
"Don't step on a frayed nerve!"

She is told there are twelve,
she has made it to the thoracic
without incident,
if she goes further to the outlying
grey swamp, branch roots,
they are there, hunched in anticipation,
she knows their tactics.

She is lucky her war is secret:
she has her clothes to hide
the scar that split her back
to deactivate bomb thirteen,
her stomach scar that cut
the blast of bomb fourteen.
She has planted warning signs:
'Must avoid the right side's peripheral nerves.'

Tonight, she will cook, read, go to bed
and sleep only on her left.

Heavy

I can see how I carry Yiayia's war
in the ample dunes of my belly,
the moment she smelt the guns,
she pinched the candle's wick,
gathered the startled shadows of her children,
flung my baby-mother onto her back
and sprinted towards the neutral moon—
that moment seeded my greed
for savaged meat, for blankets of oil
unfurled on potato and rice,
my inheritance grew by mouthfuls.

I feast on their hunger to make them proud,
so does my mother, she was spared war,
was given depression to carry
in the nerve-threaded bowls of her thighs,
arms and breasts, she reaches for the largesse
of orchards, eats the orange without pause,
staves off memories of dead fruit harvests,
swallows the threat of scurvy and anaemia   μελομακάρονα:
like *melomakarona* for morning tea.   honey soaked,
                                                 walnut-topped
Often our dinner table is dressed to please   biscuit
the gods, the saints, the prophets,
all who listened to the onslaught of prayers
before wars, between wars and after,
deep trenches are dug in my sister's stomach   φλαούνα:
to hold the children as big as *flaouna*,   cheese-filled
                                                         bread

these are our uncles and aunties
who teach her to savour the *trahana*,　　　τραχανά:
with each spoonful she incubates　　　　　grain soup
their eternal cravings.

Knock Knock

My grandmother spoke
about her time with war,
never opening the door despite
her hearth crying for company,
"Even if the voice in the dark
sounds like your neighbour's,
it could be the demon tricking
your mind into unlocking,
it could be the neighbour
who has become the enemy
while you have slept," hear
how the sound of welcome
becomes the sound of fear,
here I stand,
one side of the locked door,
noticing how my heart
is racing to open the latch
while my head is pounding
leave me alone, the knock
turns into the shrill ring into
the spill of door light's growing
spread of familiar foreign
demanding entrance, "Who's there?"

The reply is a cage of jokes
buried by ancestral warning.
The shadow grows smaller
retreats into the shape
of a shawl-covered woman,
softly hunched
opening the gate to leave
with no answer for the knock
of the world
demanding to greet
the body.

Kostaki's Harvest Woes

The soil here bleeds too
The land buries itself in your nails
It wants to teach you about the first people and their culture
But we don't listen with our pellets and blood and bone
We bring the tools of toil for another soil with its stored memories
The shovel hurts the spirits who are the true keepers of the weather
The garlic is hollow, the zucchinis are small, the tomatoes won't grow.

Each day you visit the garden like the migrant you are
You offer excuses of being fed propaganda before you arrived
The garden digs deep and yields food you won't stomach
You take off your gloves and plant your fingers to feel the pain
White soap washes the dirt, minerals, the remnants of rock.
The red iron bark will grow stronger than your lemon tree
It will tower over your house and give you permission to stay.

Looping the Waves

Admittedly, I wrestle with impatience
when Yiayia unwinds to boarding the *Patris*
"We crossed the cruel seas
to a land I couldn't pronounce."
Her flowery dialect swirls through the stagnant air,
awakens the allotted gloom
of the Glenroy nursing home,
nostalgia cranks up her cinematic eyes,
fragile hands waving in the scenes
like an over-used carousel, slide projector.
The first visual is of Yiayia at nineteen
surrounded with other pressed lips,
raised to laugh at destiny's deceit.

I stop myself mouthing the next line
falling from Yiayia's lips as easily as saliva
"Hundreds of us from cursed villages.
The sea tossed us like a salad in a bowl.
Swimming was a skill they gave to fishermen.
I prayed the sea sucked my breath while I slept.
Oh, but sleep was the lost treasure."

Yiayia grabs hold of the bedsheet
to steady her decline into the lower bunk
as the sea comes searching for memory.

This is the part when I'm meant
to play the hero, Captain Nikolaos
and take my young grandmother's hand
telling her, she will arrive safely.

Or this is the part when I'm meant
to awaken Yiayia to seventy years later,
to a room managed with programmed activity,
to unnatural light tricking the mind,
to speaking mostly to shadows.

I sit on the bunk
reach for Yiayia's quivering hand
and the old carousel continues to loop
"One man was kissing the ship's spine.
The food made me erupt, I was stuck to the ship's rail.
My vomit travelled back to slap my face."

Yiayia's words in dialect
do not dither with direction
or meaning, they sail gloriously
into inclement downpour,
navigating the deep and the shallow,
unlike Yiayia's English
drowning with confusion, searching
for the missed shore, finding
the shark infested bay.

"The water is calm, nothing to be scared of
Miss Maroulla, you can open your eyes now."
Yiayia opens her eyes and sees her Captain
smiling and says,
"Thank you for making the sea behave."

Making Lace

I see her as I see me, sitting on chairs before the impact of our craft,
both intent on making a story from a sequence, a gift out of repetition,
her stitch is my letter, her design is my phrase,
thread weave through out and in.
She is framed by a mountainous fig tree,
I have the hallway of wedding and christening photos,
her eyes meld to hands to thread to *tsimbi* to *glosi*
to caterpillar turrets to butterfly balconies
to geometrical dreamscapes of Venetian ladies
for Leonardo da Vinci to take to Rome
to robe the table for the last supper
to paint and adorn the Milan Cathedral, that is the myth from linen,
she is the story on linen,
no longer woman in small village sitting under a tree for days, months,
years of thread weave through out and in, our skin
an embroidery of old maps and new,
Lefkara, Larnaca, Kyrenia, Hartchia,
Riverwood, Bankstown, Lalor, Reservoir,
thread weave through out and in,
she lives in each strand of cotton perle, the white, brown and ecru,
she makes houses, rivers, wells, trees, caves
for secret lovers, lost children, dying soldiers,
she peeks through *gofti*, through fairy windows, and sees me,
letter by letter, crossing the keyboard
thread weave through out and in,
she sees her children's children not work in fields harvesting rotten crops,

not work in factories making hard, rough, poisonous things,
not work in shops selling dry, fried food,
she sees a series of baby girls named after her, dressed in white,
she lives in the stroke of a foreign letter by letter, word by word,
thread, weave through out and in.

tsimbi, glosi, gofti: Cypriot dialect – describing needlework techniques

Night Shift Crescendo

The rain is slapping her window
harder, harsher,
stamata, stamata   σταμάτα, σταμάτα:
                                                       stop, stop

She knows this warning well.
The wipers are trying to fend off the slaps,
pigaine piso, piso   πήγαινε πίσω:
                                                go back, back
The intersection is amber light
and proffers a U-turn
to five minutes ago,
Evans Street, Lalor, Melbourne, Australia
or five years since,
mud path, torn village, Hartchia, Cyprus.

One home has her
gulping her coffee like medicine,
covering her lips with *mavro kerasee*,   μαύρο κεράσι:
                                                    black cherry
forcing her thick curls to conform,
fighting with the shadows for her car keys,
leaving her kids to their toothpaste battles,
to their adopted bedtime stories.

Walking the dirt carpet to her tired Capri,
igniting the engine to deafen the dialect,
stile me mana   στείλε με μάνα:
                                             send me mother
Haunting the radio announcer's slumber
with the song of guilt at the village well
when water was carried like a secret lover,
stile me mana sto neron   στείλε με μάνα στο
na su do fero dhroseron   νερόν: send me to fetch
                                                 water, mother
                                           να σου το φέρω
                                    δροσερόν: I'll bring it
                                              back refreshing

The older home has crept into the car,
in the back seat, blowing into her ear
lyric, seed, graft, sprout.
"Yunaika kai sklava, bunta tha eimai."

    Γυναίκα και σκλάβα
    πάντα θα είμαι:
    A woman and slave,
    I'll always be

With the rain turning into the water
brimming with threats to spill,
stile me mana sto neron
na su do fero gatharon

    στείλε με μάνα στο
    νερόν: send me to fetch
    water, mother
    να σου το φέρω καθαρόν:
    I'll bring it back clean

There was that one path
her bare feet knew
like her mother's command,
"Pigaine yrioyra, koree mou."
And now she is stopped,
at a green light,
wanting the rain to drown
her horn of rage.

    Πήγαινε γρήγορα
    κόρη μου: Go quickly,
    my daughter

The Weed Eaters

Flower beds, vegie patches, nature strips, paved courtyards,
you are all under attack, the weeds have arrived in droves,
deep-rooting themselves in your clay-based soil,
they pretend friendship but you know they are here to compete.

I search for my tools of decapitation and, with my glove,
begin the ritual of tearing them out, they may sting, they may weep,
they may resist the tug, but I have no sympathy for their resilience
despite their appeal to my heritage of peasant foraging and eating.

Baba with his weak knees and ailing joints continues the ritual
of picking them selectively from his yard of green excess,
with his large plastic bag, seductive swing in his grip,
each nettle, thistle, dandelion, creeper and clover are his.

He offers me their contents as the world's source of wisdom
but regrets with a ragged look how to cook them like
'your mother'. I stare at them and can't see the scripture
or verse of Cyprus yet promise to keep them safe in my fridge.

At night, I can hear her robed in her silence opening the fridge.
I know what she's up to, feeding her hunger for nostalgia,
she has them cooking in my non-stick pan, then slides them
onto two plates, squeezes the lemon liberally, drizzles the oil.

Paused in the hallway, I almost return to my bed, but
her bitterness seeps in and I seek the *horta* of childhood.   χόρτα: weeds
Mama is waiting. We eat as one, ravenous for what was.

The Good Citizens of Melbourne

"Trams are the good citizens of Melbourne ... There are nearly 700 trams on Melbourne streets. Looking after them takes a lot of men: cleaners, overhaulers, tradesmen of all sorts ..."

Citizen Tram, a 1960s film by The Melbourne and Metropolitan Tramways Board

Sitting next to my young mother is Deena, her sister
with eyes men fall into.
She's older and focused on
getting them to work,
making sure they don't miss
stop 20.   Facing her
but almost falling into her lap is Thelema, her cousin
with arms and legs that don't stop talking:
"Did you hear about Effie? Yes, you know her,
she's the one with the glass eye,
the one that works the zipper machine,
she's fifteen, younger than me – she looks fifty.
She has a *proxenia*,   προξενιά: arranged marriage
he's at least thirty,
her parents want to get rid of her
because of the *zeemia*   ζημιά: trouble in the sense of scandal
with the gelato shop boy."
With a slight lean of her head
away from the window
Deena intervenes,
"Effie shouldn't be forced,
it's criminal, her parents are *varvaroi!*"   βάρβαροι: barbarians

Then my mother, who is a mere fifteen herself
says, "Maybe she's better off,
who wants to be *sklavos*   σκλάβος: slave (worker)
for the rich man
and his needle and thread machine?"

Deena, Thelema, Young Mum are
a trio of handbags, lunch boxes,
orange, apricot, lavender skirts,
shirts with wide, white collars
showing neck bones, smiles
of modest pink lipstick,
earrings that clasp the ear tight,
knees protruding with pent up
bursts of freedom as they speak
in a flurry of Cypriot-Greek
on a busy tram
heading to a factory
where young women
make fashion
for others.

The tram
halts
before stop 20,
the Driver
turns his mouth into a fist,
"On this tram we speak English
if you keep up with your gibberish
you can get off at the next stop!"

The language hovers over their heads
like a thought cloud of *orexee*,   όρεξη: appetite
dark spiralling,   (enthusiasm, initiative)
sending them down into a well
where there are no windows to see
the plum trees, the magpies, the milkbars.
Each day they caught that tram
they renewed their vow
of silence.

Incident in Aisle 5

I was almost as tall as the shopping trolley,
I could see up and through its bars
to catch the slap of Mama's hate
across Baba's cheek.
What's he done this time?
A question on loop.
Her purse was agape,
not one coin.
The trolley was a foolish promise
of fruit cups, Weetbix, raisin toast.

His cheeks were a permanent red,
genetic markers of so … so …
sorry, shoulders tilted to grovel,
suspicion arose
if something came good.

She swiped my hand off the trolley,
zipped her bag shut and marched
down the aisle
without one look back.

He continued to search the floor
for answers.
I knew she would leave
expecting me to follow,
I ran after her—
I did turn once
and saw a man
on his knees
between the Corn Flakes and the Milo
transfixed to that trodden floor.

Kostaki's Signature

Hard to believe those five hacked clumps
could produce an intricate dance of highs
and lows of circles and spirals then stop
like quick death. I thought I knew this man.

He grew me on meat, bread and stories
of him. His best friend, the knife
taught him to carve away from the bone,
the secrets of sea flesh, kept him alive.

He told me the pen was skittish at first
and how he practised words to seduce
this shapeless slippery spill of mess
to make his name valued on paper.

He left this dance for me to imitate
on tissue box, doily, napkin, table,
his expression of a second life
on visa, passport, license, home loan.

Fatigue

They come with sweets and flowers, sometimes with shopping vouchers.
They want to know about my experience of hate since I've arrived.
Have I been tempted to walk without my hijab outside?
Has my pram been jostled by white elbows and knees?
Have I thrown my phone into the bin to stop
the onslaught of trolls?
I say *No* but my body says *Yes.*
They come again with longer questions
to ascertain my resilience or resistance.
These questions are like homework from a school
in a language I've never been taught.
Last night these questions entered my dreams,
I was fighting them like thirsty mosquitos.

The flowers were the bright *Hello* of my internal smile
when I walked the safe streets those first months.
My flowers now are sick with grief,
each question asks me to reach down into my bowels
to vomit the despair I wish I'd drown.
If I answer truthfully they promise to advocate.
I am wading in deep water already.
How many answers before my head is immersed?

If I had their ease with English,
I would write their report
without the data, category or diagnosis,
it would be the story of the woman
who thought she would never fear
tolerance.

Inner Sense

as-salaam alaykum
At the entrance, shoes are parked
in casual companionship,
colour, fabric, tone,
mingle among frayed labour,
special occasion and home comfort.

Closer I can read the journey of each sole,
the imprint of working this weekend
at Tibe's bakery, of 'falling' for Elias,
of getting 89 for linear maths,
which isn't 98 but one day—

I take off my shoes, there is a space
next to a pair of pink-buckled clogs,
they welcome my shoes with her story.
She arrived from Iran two years ago,
the Australian language is not the English
she was taught, she secured a job
as a 'multicultural officer', the mosquitoes
drink her skin, she's developed hives.

wa alaykum as-salaam
I walk barefoot
towards prayers
collected from shoulder to shoulder
hoping to see Rana
to show her my bitten arm
as if it was her arm,
"Mozzies love us and hate us!"
she says.
I share with her the cream
I've found
that seems
to soothe.

An Extracurricular Assessment

Sharif's eyes were wild with outrage
at my father's admission of fear,
it took less than two minutes to know
Sharif would never be offered
coffee or tea in my parents' house,
Mama was wearing her apron
like an Orthodox robe,
refusing to sit at the kitchen table,
language graduated swiftly
from denial to refusal,
Baba raised a finger like a slap
at the language of values
being tested by this boy
from university
whom his daughter sat next to
with reckless abandon
for her life, her church, her soul.
My eyes fixed on Mama's fingers
fidgeting like captured birds
inside the deep pocket of her apron
while, under the table, my hand
gripped Sharif's thigh
to steady our fall.

Unlike the shrewd wise men
who planned their travel
and their gifts,
I ignored the cross
made from dried grass,
threaded through the bars
of their screen door;
their makeshift scarecrow.

I delivered to them
a Muslim
wrapped in a love
torn
by conquerors and wars,
by words in a birth-marked book,
by years of stab or run.

The English Missionary

She extended her arm like a lead
and I, being trained to obey
knew we would end in the scolding room
where her tone would inflict
the ruler's sharp pain across knuckle.

My body inclined to her tendency,
it knew to brace and restrain
to pretend remorse with blushed cheeks,
eyes lowered to her heels, to curate
my shadow in the shape of supplicant.

I preferred this exercise
as new words flew into my face
like 'insolence' and 'impertinence'.

Her other practice
brought true disease to my heart,
when she used her thick ink pen
to rape
the careful planting
of my letter by letter,
of my word by word,
the careful creation of my sentence
turning into the wonder of the paragraph
into the miracle of the story
to make sense
of me.

Kinaesthetic Grace

This woman talks to me with her hands
she always has, since birth
I have failed to grasp them.
I have followed the voices and text
I've found outside the home,
words on pages in whatever language, discipline or culture
bound by libraries,
left this woman to create her own story
with soil and seeds, flour and salt,
a cloth, a needle, a pot, an oven
her fingers are an alphabet
I had no patience for.

This is the woman who knows how to hold
with her lined and stained hands
the story of all other women
we service with a system of pay-outs,
women of colour on the General Motors assembly line
playing the conveyor belt like an instrument
they will never learn,
Hispanic women wearing paper masks as they spray
jeans and their lungs into shreds,
her fingers twitch when they tell
of the Thomastown factory's sewing machine,
stitch by never-ending stitch,
bleeding before a stop for break,
the dip and throb of migraine fighting quota.
This is the woman
silenced by statistics.

We must search for her
not in photo albums nor newspapers,
we must go out to the wild woods
where there are trees left to grow old,
like hunting for prized truffles,
we must smell, touch, taste,
and when we see her
hold out our hands
as children willing to learn.

Coburg

The laneways are made of your lashes and muscle
I know because I have walked the length of your torso
I have felt the bluestone under my bare feet
The strength of your values that pave my path
The butterfly brush against my thigh as I step
toward the gentle hurt of your childhood scars.

You have entered my heart through my craving
for your delicate drizzle, slow sooth kneading
as you turn a street of falafel, pita, zaatar, mannoush
into our wedding aisle, with the music of *True North*
lifting me to share your thirst for the local brew,
falling head-first into you, my reticent, urban lake.

When Coburg Lake Became a Kyrenia Wedding

The way the water is quiet, the cool touch of the willows,
geese get all snappy when you get too close,
leaves cling to the branches as the wind hums
the song of a fisherman's son, who once travelled the oceans
to stand forty years later, hand-in-hand with his love
as she sees the harbour and his father's trawler
arrive with the catch for their wedding feast.

She feeds the ducks the song of summer's light,
toasts their hunger with haloumi, pita, salata,
he sails his handkerchief, the one stitched by his mother
with the Greek letter Kappa, across their heads
it ripples like a flag of surrender, settles and frames them
as Nostalgia and Memory—married till death.
You will find them swaying by the edge of the lake.

When the Hills Hoist Became the Wishing Tree

With a peg in her mouth,
Maroulla walks the circumference of the 'clothes tree'
looks at each pillowcase, sheet, tablecloth, Taki's singlet,
reminders of the white handkerchiefs
tied to the wishing tree at Paphos.

When she was eight, she tried to reach the branch
with her hanky,
there was no one there to hold her up,
she didn't whisper her secret dream to the tree that day
and the next morning she left,
stuffing her flag of surrender
into her suitcase.

Taki's out for the day,
she's alone
with her waving, white promises,
she touches them one by one,
the pillowcase, sheet, tablecloth — his singlet.

She reaches and holds onto the bar,
swings herself into the wind,
at peace with spent wishes and dreams.

She is a flying stream of coral, rose and black,
she is laughter spilling itself into the sun,
she is the fragile wires of affection,
she has come to know
as home.

Outskirts

Soon she will know when to jump as the path erupts
into rubble and weeds, she will neglect to jolt
as she passes the brick veneer with its outbursts
of Persian by the truck driver without driver's license,
won't cringe at the window of the clinker brick
when the woman with smudged eyes, wearing belly and bra
blows smoke to follow her like a neighbourhood pest.

She will not count the nineteen train stations
like a word-count of labour for an essay on torts,
won't look at the perpetual fight between art and defiance
on the ocean of walls riding the train's tracks,
won't read the history of her upbringing as a textbook
to carry from one lecture to the other on precedent.

She will sit among a hierarchy of chairs before a human lectern,
grip her pen as it speeds across the page to catch the lofty Latin,
hold her tongue as the Dean speaks, with no doubt
"To make a difference is to obey the rules." She learns
clauses, sections, caveats are the ripples among the waves
to reach those boats collapsing with the effort of hope.

The Quadrangle of Dreams

*The Melbourne University Law School buildings
were constructed in 1854–57*

First Day
The calendar insisted it was summer and yet
it was bone deep cold
standing cloaked in grey
before the arch and its parade of cloisters,
frantically searching among
my sinews and nerves
for the grandeur of spirit
to enter and walk
through the crowded silence
of those competing centuries.

Second Day
A paralysed pause
before the sandstone eminence,
last night it opened
to become the cave of treasure
then grew a tongue and teeth
to swallow my baby
I christened *Potential*.
The wind comes to greet me
like forced friendship
Postera crescam laude
shaking my body
expecting me to become
the university's motto
before I'm permitted within.

Day after day
I prefer to run through the quad
after my mandatory pause at the arch,
there come the echoes to chase me
past the vaulting until the annex
with its spill of green-light laughter
where I'm escorted by the dead,
the honours students,
to those parts of the library
inhaling their breath.

To Identify the Apostate

All avoid drowning in the lecturer's drone
by taking perfunctory notes,
each with note pad and textbook,
positioned slightly to the left
to write with the right.

I cultivate worry with my left,
always the apologetic spill,
the readjustment of tools
to accommodate the right.

In earlier years, I complied,
held the pen with the hand
of redemption,
became a stumbling fool on the page
which made me run back to my left,
cursed with ill-omen, and yet
became the fluid dancer of arabesque
with cursive pirouettes.

I remember waddling
with my left hand strapped to my back
by Mama, enthused with the Orthodox parable
> *The shepherd divideth his sheep from the goats.*
> *Jesus said unto man, to my right are the sheep*
> *who will inherit the kingdom of God,*
> *to my left are the goats, depart from me,*
> *ye cursed, into everlasting fire.*
I search among the sheep, the bees, the ants
for goats, each day,
I assimilate my allotted space,
note pad and book slightly to my right,
left elbow constrained like a goat's horn,
browse the page, devour each point
and know I'm marked from birth.

Goddess Nike

I sit among the common characters
the clown, the fidget, the stirrer,
somewhere in the middle row
where I'm a head with no name,
five rows behind the pantheon
who arrive on clouds,
their tongues like swords
swift to strike down
any insolence.

Puzzled by their exclusivity,
their inability to see each student
is a family, a community, a country.

One of them is winged
and grazes on silver and ice leftovers,
intent on battle to prove her point,
she lifts a hand to fire an arrow
at the lecturer, creates a blast wave
of angry doodles, the war begins.

Somewhere Overseas

There is a woman in a bedsit
six flights, fourteenth door
living in silence she writes
"If my world is my thoughts on paper
then contentment is surely accessible"
split curtain exposes
the same sky for the next woman
in the makeshift canopy of crestfallen dresses
twisted to earth like sandbags in trenches
she writes
"… but contentment is a greater place
than a hometown
and world knowledge should be
a first-hand experience"
looking up
at the bang of blue
shared with the next woman
in the steel bar basement,
a concrete pillow to bed her diary
she writes "… the emphasis of experience
is what I need to convince people"
the clouds tumble in a wake of shadows
for the next woman
with a bay-view alcove of manicured roses
who writes
"… to convince myself of my own validity
is the greatest battle."

The Colour Chase

Krishna took off his robe and wished
it was his skin he could remove,
it was a dark blue,
he would never have chosen,
if only he could be fair like Radha

        I heard the banging of drums
        before I saw the Nepalese woman
        swollen with child
        running towards me
        splattered like a Jackson Pollock
        ecstasy encased her face
        intent on throwing *abeer*
        I instigated a chase down the hill
        thinking I would win
        given I had gravity on my side

Krishna could choose
whatever colour he wanted
to change Radha,
he thought of red then green
but settled on blue
so she would know his pain

        With legend and ritual on *her* side
        she caught up when I tripped
        and flung the red powder
        like a blanket on fire,
        it covered my face and arms,
        I was no longer me
        but a symbol of love
        and like her,
        a vessel for birth

Radha looked in the mirror
and saw her skin was equal to Krishna's
what an honour, she thought,
my skin shows
the temper of sky and sea,
the eternal unrest of power.

Shanker Hotel, New Delhi, 1991

It's not always the same man knocking
coaxing with kind English or high-pitch,
testing the lock with a shoulder, a knife,
the knock turns into bang,
to Hindi outrage with thrust,
the door becomes compromised,
shifts towards their effort.
I have the company of four stained walls,
Shiva is hanging lopsided,
the bed, the floor, the heat say,
"This is your room service."
I search for the branch from the Jamun tree,
use my shaver to sharpen its tip,
stand still as my heart sobs, screams,
I am thankful for the bars across the window,
I am thankful for no balcony,
I beg the door to hold its stance
as I stand, I am statue of myth or legend
holding the branch like the upward sword
held by Maroula of Lemnos
who won the attack
despite the army of men
barging through doors
to rape her island.

'How to Drape a Saree'
Bhagwanlila Exports, Varanasi, India

With a blouse and petticoat on,
hold the end border
in your left hand
and wrap it around
your waist.

> With shy hands, I opened the tissue paper
> to show Amir the rich blue silk and gold trim
> of something his mother and sisters
> would wear with ease and comfort.

Thrust the said end
inside the right upper
end of the petticoat
and gather it about you
nicely as you thrust
again into the petticoat.

> Amir said his father would be appeased,
> but his mother would find something wrong
> about how I wore it or the colour I chose,
> to avoid drama, wear my Western skirt.

Wrap it around your waist
up to the armpit of your
right arm, as you hold it by
the left hand whilst
pulling and pleating
by the right hand
for a smart look.

          With silent stares, they scream 'wrong'
          at my display of inexact skin
          and the way the hem fails to flare
          as I trip on my rehearsed words

Finally, rest the excess
across and over your left shoulder
allow it to drape
and swing wide
over your backside.

          It's Amir's sister who gently opens the door
          to see my battle with tears and mascara
          she finds a washcloth, and with careful English
          she helps me to remember who *I* am.

The Summit of Choice

She is sitting on the edge of a mountain in the Annapurna,
her face, away from the camera,
her gaze, focused on the Lamjung peak,
experiencing a moment of peace
like many before and many after,
the seconds could be hours could be days,
the weather could be challenging or kind,
she could be alone or surrounded by trekkers,
it has taken careful hoarding of time and money
to be sitting there framed by sky and snow
hardly a foot away from death,
thinking of nothing and everything,
feeling No God and All God,
standing up, leaping forward,
standing up, going back,
she is sitting on the edge of a mountain in the Annapurna,
she has crossed a rhododendron forest,
held tightly to the rails of a rickety bridge
overlooking the Marsyangdi River,
she has passed through mud floor, village huts,
compared her mountain boots to Sherpa's sandals,
guilt and shame have sunk into her breastbone,
her body with its frozen toe, altitude migraine, whimpering stomach
has acclimatised to gratitude
for the nourishment of dal,
for the breath of pure air,
for the joy of one step after the other,
back home, she was told to strive for Everest,

the one with knife like peaks, aligned with Western quest
to scale the top at cost of health and ego,
she is sitting on the edge of a mountain in the Annapurna,
her cup of contentment continues to be filled and emptied
by her Nepalese mentor
who talks the view into experience of light and dark
of how the lower range brings the cradle of shade
to nurture you as "the child you must become."

Travel with a Coward's Heart

As I walked from the adobe house to the welded gate
enclosing an ancient chorus of forced starvation,
described as a 'Tucson garden',
I ingested the penetrating stares
of the saguaro cacti,
their shadows cast a march of giants
who swallowed my attempt to lean with my chest.

It may have been the silence of those guns
hanging from the porches like Christmas baubles,
the sinister shutters closing their eyes,
the thud of ghost cowboy boots—
a spook circled my vertebrae
smoking the cigar of untimely death.

I thought I mastered the language of listen,
knew how to inhale difference better than air,
between rib cage and breastbone
I had the happy lumps of adventures
circa 1991
on a motorbike speeding through New Delhi,
trekking the Annapurna and sleeping among
constellations of accent and dialect.

Thirty years later, 'warning' stitches my skin,
nerves of ancestral wars quilted to bones of daily news,
alarms, alerts, rations, curfews,
these threads twist into narrative and history,
into a rush to retrace my steps.

Abduction

She is cooking walleye for supper
intent on making fish familiar to my birthland,
minute by minute she becomes my other mother
and I become the baby, learning without choice.
She calls me, "the daughter I wanted to have."
I shape my words to fit her vowels, rehearse the lines
to walk the new planet of strange gestures
that I'm told mean love.

Her backyard isn't concrete holding a Hills hoist
of damp sheets, it is pine trees, a hammock, a pier
leading to a lake called Gull, and a pontoon.
I sit on an iron-sleeper at the edge of the pier
look out to the stretch of ever-blue
imagine toddling towards the horizon
each new step becomes her accent
until our voices are married.

Across Gull Lake I hear
the sound of the solitary loon's
haunting call,
"Come to me, come to me"
my heart flies back to Melbourne,
"Come to me, come to me"
I am running, running as fast as my little legs
will take me, back to the brick house
with the concrete yard,
safe for me to play
skippy and knucklebones.

Calling

January 2009
Maroulla makes her nest
out of 82 years
of threaded memory, cobwebbed hope,
there is no space to sit on the edge of her bed
of worship to ripped letters
of long-ago love,
bracelets, cups, spoons, scarves
the treasure of tea chests and drawers
spread over her bed to recall their use,
each hand-picked photo is the quilted album
of grow, escape, arrive, settle,
her hand darts to the strand of blue-eyed worry beads,
each bead is cradled like a grandchild in a ceremony
of sacred water.

January 2010
Maroulla's carer speaks,
hysteria fanning her voice,
"Your Grandmother … calling your name."
I run, I drive, dread suffocating my heart.
The carer holds me away from the room,
"Better to remember her—"
The smell is the candle left burning
to flame the nest into a silent war—
the victor is not the fire,
it is the poem of the ritual
naming the child
to honour the past.

Good Night

1993,
I walked the night
through Alma Park, St Kilda, from 10 pm
to 4 am, no chaperone, no iPhone,
the poetry gig would end,
I would leave,
take the tram,
no taxi, no text-talk, no self-talk
and walk
for blocks
through city lanes, urban parks, industrial streets,
half a city and two suburbs of walking
to clear the day's debris.

It was night who befriended me
when my house was slashing and stabbing,
I kept clear of the family room,
unpacked my tantrums
with insomniacs, nurses
and night-feeders.

2019, I walk
with no moon for witness,
my steps are the loud protest,
I hear muffled blasts
of his outrage,
her resentment,
in a house I pass.

A hunched figure
sparks the path,
slows down
to show
a girl.

We nod
like soldiers
at the frontline.

Frontline

Some stories remain like bruises,
others are bullets, those told
with fear pounding the phone.
There is the breath you listen for as well as the word,
each one counts, the breath, the word, the breath.
Allow the story to battle itself into existence.
The woman is all ages, she is all colours,
both rich and poor, able to dodge grenades
run, hide, implode with the word, the breath, the word.
Erin, Poppy, Franka, Nivy   whisper, sob, scream
reliving their trigger into the phone
"His eyes get that way
the smell of his sick mouth
Charlie crying and crying for a feed
me unable to get up
my blouse a mess of milk and blood."
Where is the breath?

There is history
compounding their words,
I hear their mothers
and their mothers' mothers'
their words are carefully placed
between each
and every breath
they have fought
to possess
for so long.

The line is attacked
during times families are told
to expect gifts and joy,
children's voices raise the alarm
"Mum get off the phone, he's in the garage!"
entrenched,
pores on the alert, they throw a flare
"Will anyone, please pick up?"
Many abandon the queue,
willing to go missing in action,
fifteen seconds is always too late.

It's getting dark, the phone is ringing,
the woman is saying, sorry, sorry, over and over.
"There is no one to tell,
I want to talk but I can't."
We can breathe together, I say and we do.
When she is ready, she will tell me her story.
At the end, she will hang up.
I will gather her story, gently in my arms, sing to it
the song of honour and courage,
wrap it in a shroud and place it alongside
the rows and rows and rows —

Yiayia is Swimming in my KeepCup

"… none of us leaves our personal stuff at the door, that we are always seeking to replicate structures from our childhood … we can each do our work but not expect the organization to solve the wounds of our childhood."

Jerry Colonna, Podcast,
Can you really bring your whole self to work?

From my spinal cord the spirited child
swings up through my lungs
and leaps from my mouth
with words like unruly curls,
despite my hair stretched into submission,
and pale blue, buttoned-up shirt
defying my grandmother's colours of roar and bleed.

The child is listening to Yiayia	Γιαγιά: Grandmother
as the data morphs into ena dyo tria	ένα δύο τρία: One two three
as the fluorescent light holds a firm, old hand	
resting on my shoulder	
reminding me to eat my lunch.	

Ee glossa tis miteras   Η γλώσσα της μητέρας:
wafts from my moussaka   the mother tongue
disturbing those lunch packs
with food of calm and order,
my language of birth
with values to live
and reasons to die
sits hunched
as if tending to an open fire, as if
retrieving water from a smelly well,
my legs fated to walk uphill
even in stockings and heels.

At branch meetings
all staff are grafted
to their family's tree,
their words drop like fruit
from the lips of the dead,
their ideas no more than
leaves of retired ancestors.

She travels the length of my report
using pen to mark her birth tongue,
scolds with her dead father's voice,
"Critical deficiencies in negotiation,"
he enjoys squeezing her soul.

Australia Visits Minnesota

January 2020
There are two main types of snow,
one slices skin, pierces organs, pretends friendship and fun,
the other falls gently into submission, curls into the folds of embrace,
forms the smile to frame nostalgia.
I walk in snow to forget the other half of my face
staring at the blaze running towards the verandah.
This snow shares the air produced
by two nuclear plants,
five million heaters and hearths,
a smoke snaking itself across the equator,
particles feel like grit in our teeth.
Coughing comes in cold and hot weather,
it carries our conversations,
stalks our voices.

Regulation

The haze tends towards insomnia,
giddy with release,
celebrating the new year's red moon,
it will not race you to the bus
this morning, you have time to breathe,
still, wear your runners,
walk like you're about to jog.
Don't close your gate, you may need to return
before you arrive.
There is talk of the older eucalypt
heaving with the weight of ash —
do not seek its shelter,
keep away from its outstretched branches,
keep up your pace
as the haze will wake
its smoke to play
the game of seek, find, choke.
Do not take off your mask
to wipe your sweat,
keep your ears alert,
do not fill with plugs to avoid
the subtle crackle and creak
of earth and air
in hot contest
for your life.

The Daily Commute

Up till 15 March 2020
This train carried a marketplace of colour and language,
it was the variety of skin from deep-texting black
to the open call of brown, and my skin
with its comments on weather and work
was there, as not-quite-white with the moles and freckles
colliding into a marriage of Mediterranean sun.
We sat uncaged, could touch each other's shoulder,
smell the accent of breakfast, the craving for lunch.
Remember Anisa Zahidee, not quite 30 with two degrees
and a bag full of books, Hidayet Ceylan knew her,
sat next to her, asked her out once,
she politely declined, they still talked,
he knew some Farsi, she knew some Turkish,
created a dance of words with English falling in
at each stop to remind us we were driven
and our worth was pre-sold.

From 5 April 2020
Woman 1 is sitting front seat with her back
to Woman 2 who sits mid-carriage
away from Only Man in the corner watching.
Woman 1 is wearing surgical mask.
Only Man is wearing white cotton mask.
Woman 2 is wearing bandanna over her mouth.
The train's engine is the monologue of screech
you can hear at a nurses' desk when they call
the names after hours of waiting, the test
is not to sneeze or cough between stops,
to hold breath as you look out the window
at lonely bike paths and roads, the test
is not to look at the face of the other
to work out the colour, the language,
to unearth the story of why, where
and for how long?

Father

Your blue and red lights scale the length of your arms
raised as they are to the darkening sky,
I remember the muscle-bound, stubborn build of years
learning your grid of conformity.

Swanston, Lonsdale, Bourke   pulsing your veins,
fueled by a rev to grow each laneway
into a European chorus of table wine,
how you basked in your popularity,
gripped the values of strangers, the emotions of family,
turned them into the hoard of guest
drinking the undercurrent of your flushing fountain.

Now with windows pained and blinking lament
you seek my awe of your history,
the way I sat caged to your open-plan view,
huddled in the spine of routine,
your nose hooked by crane to scrape the sky
flares with squalor at your feet,
sniffs with petrol at my car-flung distance.

If I told you of walks to see water escaping,
eucalypts determined to touch clouds,
nature strips turned into miniature forests,
the lacework of wisteria's shadow, would
you stop spruiking your dense arterials?

We did share nostalgia for ambling conversations
as we rode the escalator's waves,
you procured stories from abseiling cleaners
to coach our vertical survival,
and you returned the statues, balconies and turrets
to the homeless pigeons.

But then came your cladding to hide welts from burns,
the white-knuckle, scaffold race,
draining the breath of air between us — Father
I hear your whistle through your fractured walkways,
please don't expect me to visit.

Homework

Stretch your arms beyond their length
to hold the breadth of your mind's office
as you convert your kitchen to cook
the ingredients of *zoom* and *trello*
for board meeting appetites,
tested recipes sprinkled
with agenda and timelines.

Envy and confusion play squash
in walls plastered for family living
with monitors dressed like dinner plates,
cords for cutlery, keyboards for food
and a pre-supper screening
of your after-hours colleague
devouring a grape.

Back in the day, the man of the house
would spread his legs under the mahogany desk
as big as a boat to sail his intimacy
to the isolated coast of hubris.

Today, you will find the son sits with his mum
within ear-shot of genetic groans as dad paces
with headphones to the off-beat of a daily check-in
addressing his spatula to flip the omelette.

Each day, parents and children race as they recline
in slippers with hair pampered by pillow,
peppered with sleep pips they mute
the growls of belly, the grunts of bum,
clicking with the speed of a morning dream,
they wear a smile in time to greet
small portraits who float into view
and speak like guests
invited to dine.

The Guest

My arms ache from the strain of holding her
far enough
to scan my daily walk
from kettle to couch, toaster to desk, laundry to clothesline.

She birthed me through marriage
our love
is sifted with politeness,
she ignores my moth-eaten raisin-toast, the crusted frypan.

My ghosts of philoxenia
berate me
as I steer her fossicking eyes away
from failure to preserve my fig tree's burst of excess.

We built a routine on airport hugs
spent years
of salary without guilt, swapped like gifts
museums, galleries, mountain walks, shopping malls.

A state, a continent, an equator
collapse
as I plunge her into lukewarm coffee
watching her bake sticky-date buns, I once devoured.

Sometimes her face freezes
on death
as our Earth curls itself into the ten steps
from my side-gate to her backyard.

Shelter

We are the travellers of small steps
wearing pyjamas and slippers
to greet each room as if it were a country
encountered from a plane flight,
konnichiwa to the space called Living
ola to the island called Kitchen
ni hao to the mattress of pent up dreams,
in the study there is the desk
holding geography's memory,
salve, kalimera, take me with you.

My mother will be lighting her candles
on her bench-top to create her church,
my father will shuffle with his frame
to the chair on the porch with the vista
of his twelve-year-old eyes diving
for sea sponges from an unsteady pier.

This space termed *Home*
is a document of journey
as we come to know the walls as trees
we long to climb,
the doors to close or open
depending on altitude and inclement,
the ceiling will seem higher than Everest,
from the carpet we see the grit
of hiking through jungle.

And there, in the lonely corner
is the blue rug to sit on and breathe in
the smell of the ocean calling its waves
to sweep our dust.

After Dinner

7.50 pm, 3 August 2020, Coburg, Victoria

Her name is Filomena, I call her Fil,
strangers and reporters call her Pyjama Mama

one night, after rinsing and stacking the dishes,
she sprayed Lemon Myrtle throughout the house

fear continued to permeate the living room
as the news spread its grime all over her couch

that night, she didn't sync her iphone into doom-scroll,
she failed to perform her part in the family's chorus

she didn't sneak nor march towards the front door,
it was as casual as going to the shop for bread

at first, the silence was gun fire — startling,
there were no cars charging the street like a red flag

the ambulance siren was a sweet whistle of care,
the night sky was an empty casket of dreams

and she walked in the middle of her street
with spotted zebras nibbling night's air.

8.05 pm, 8 September 2020, Coburg, Victoria

She keeps walking in her pink bunny slippers
passes the red post-box, turns into Lever Street

as if pulled by a thought, another follows her
with lip-stick poodles pattering the breeze

flannel carves their bodies into canvasses
of cotton creatures rippling with joy

another middle-aged mother, another woman
with a computer fighting with laundry-time

they become the neighbourhood's lullaby,
an unrehearsed choreography of comfort

pink tigers, red pandas, stripes and swirls
follow the poodles, following the zebras

through a grid of carved bitumen and grass,
their slippers silence the day's crescendo.

8.35 pm, 30 September 2020, Coburg, Victoria

The wind slaps our faces, twists our hair,
dogs lunge at us through ravaged fences

the moon cowers as a tree grows arms,
even then, we are like posties or soldiers

we are the mothers feeding the night
with our milk curing sores and aches

our walk is an allegory before bedtime,
a sip of chamomile with port or whisky

unlike our day made of survival's tenets,
there is no talk to drill rules into hearts

Fil is our quiet, useful bookmark
turning each street into a page

as we pass, some windows offer
clues to once-upon-a-time.

8.45 pm, 16 October 2020, Coburg, Victoria

the boundary road is never crossed,
it's our river Lethe, our warning

a semi-trailer blares its horn of stress,
we recall a key used to ignite speed

we circle back carrying our animals
as dreams designed to coax sleep.

Diagnoses

In the mirror there is no sign of war
yet it's been raging for years
and like 'fake news' the shallow skin
continues the charade of existence.

There is no need to dig a deep trench
into the torso, just fix your ear
and you will hear the off-beat blasts
no heart can control.

My condition is your fixation
you have delivered papers on its catastrophic outbursts
when it escapes the mutilated body
to hurl words of threat and conquer.

Honour me with *your* secret
as you walk home from your office
to settle your head by lamp light,
tell us how your body executes your mind.

Remission

Mama is waiting for me perched on her cliff
with her black, bat-winged parasol opened
scrutinising the sky with owl spectacles,
there might be sun that sears our backs,
there could be rain dropping pellets,
she has thoughtfully dressed
in a light fabric, hewn from the temerity
of leaves from all seasons,
the young green cleave to the bodice,
weaved in with the creases and crinkles
of fallen and rested,
needled into the flow of the skirt and sleeves.

These days she is so easy to carry,
her 75 years of story and lamentation
fold into the contours of my back
becoming my carapace as I stretch my neck
towards the horizon of densely designed
scaffolds and cranes holding the steel
and concrete blocks,
we scale as one species.

It is only when we reach the turret
of "Yiatrina"   Γιατρίνα: The female doctor
she disembarks to unveil
her ruptured, heroic body
awakened from death

by telescopic insistence,
Mama looks to me to voice her gratitude
and acceptance, as I become the myth
of the humble whisperer
'upon settlement in strange land'.

After the tick of health,
Mama would rather I climb her back
but her carapace shrank into her spine
when she turned 51,
and we both know that my heart
was birthed for two souls.

Through pathways spilling cables like entrails,
she screams in fear of our fall
until we reach the turbulent weeds near home,
where she dares her body to escape my back
and trudges the climb with nose to the ground,
as if a mushroom would sprout with a sniff,
her memory creeps and entangles
my feet to her door,
she implores me to enter
with a fig she snatched from a passing branch,
knowing I am now the eight-year-old
with the hunger for anything sweet.

2020

This is the year of cross-stitch steps,
no large leap for mankind teaches
anything known or new, small is

the bounty of the meek, each step
an abundance of life and death,
each stitch is a step from backdoor

to fence, the stitch from clothesline to
carport, the step to fishbone fern,
the stitch to Araneae's nest   look

this is our garden's festival
of earth spirits swimming, flying,
floating to galaxies unknown.

Ocean View

The path of steady shifted to crumbling
rock, clinging to the rails,
my age was no longer a division of stories
easily mapped with tales of strife,
since birth, my skin, an erosion
of views by Eleni and Kostaki,
overseen by Orthodox scripture
counting the remainder
as children   always.

The trail walk was advertised with swell,
a confluence of cottage flowers
and balconies with views
to open like presents under trees
that never die.

I clenched the rails with each step,
wanting to swallow the view
as teenager leaving home
but found the sea's mirror.

I saw grey hair slapping the wind
with arms strong and swift
welded to a knife and the twist
of shell hardened with bearded sea dregs,
with the ebb of calcified grit.

This Yiayia continued to wrestle the shell
for the soft life within, the need
to slurp the phlegm of Poseidon
with a drop of lemon, hint of salt,
taste of regret.

Abundance

Those spaces named house, office, tower
we can visit
after the war, the plague, the fire,
bullets rested with stained blankets with charred stoves
with quiet reprieve,
they will proudly show us what they've made
out of the damp, from the debris, by the dusk,
these things we left to perish
entwine like a thick braid.
See how the springs are now free
from the burden of mattress,
how passionfruit tendrils weave in and out
of the coils, offering their purple bloom.
As if music has entered their souls,
chairs topple over each other
dancing to gravity and flight,
no longer weighted with the heft of routine.
Each step we make is applauded
with an echo made from walls
allowed to grow their own skin,
to breathe their own smells.

Notes

Some of the poems contain Cypriot dialect or Greek words and they are translated alongside the poem or after the poem. Often these words are phonetically written to keep to the metre or rhythm of the poem.

Yiayia: Γιαγιά: Grandmother in Greek. Referring to my maternal and paternal grandmothers and ties to other grandmothers through kinship and travel to Cyprus, listening to their oral stories.

Mama: Μαμά: Mother in Greek.

Baba: Μπαμπά: Father in Greek.

Heavy (page 6)
melomakarona: a honey-soaked biscuit, infused with chopped walnuts, made by Cypriots and Greeks.

flaouna: a plump cheese and herb-filled bread made by Cypriots for Greek Orthodox Easter.

trahana: a Cypriot soup made from a dried, fermented mixture of grain and yogurt, strained tomatoes, and pieces of haloumi cheese. It is a weighty soup, filling like porridge.

Making Lace (page 13)
to *tsimbi* to *glosi*: [literally] narrow or wide; the reference is to Lefkara embroidery in Cyprus, where linen cloth is embroidered with traditional motifs and the lacework around the edges can be either fine and narrow (*tsimbi*) or wider in design (*glosi*). These are rare Cypriot dialect words.

Lefkara, Larnaca, Kyrenia, Hartchia,: these are towns and villages of Cyprus; the first two are known for producing intricate embroidery for tables and dressers, while the last two are known for their harbour and port and, since 1974, are situated in the Turkish-occupied part of Cyprus.

gofti: a term used by Cypriot-Greek lace makers to refer to the holes they embroider in their intricate work, likened to 'little windows for fairies'. Again, a rare Cypriot dialect word.

Night Shift Crescendo (page 15)
Parts of a classic Cypriot song are threaded: Send me mother... Send me for water, mother, do, I'll bring it back so cool for you... Send me for water, mother, do, I'll bring it back so clean for you.

The Weed Eaters (page 17)
horta is a Greek word and a reference to certain weeds eaten by Cypriots and Greeks. A traditional village dish.

Inner Sense (page 24)
On 15 March 2019, my Muslim friends were shattered by the horrific massacre by one lone gunman of Muslims in prayer at Christ Church, New Zealand. As a way of healing, 50 shoes were painted white for each life taken.

as-salaam alaykum is a greeting in Arabic often used by Muslims, which means 'peace be upon you'.

wa alaykum as-salaam is a greeting in Arabic often used by Muslims, which in essence means 'and unto you peace'.

Kinaesthetic Grace (page 29)
DeGraffenreid v General Motors Assembly Div., *United States District Court for the Eastern District of Missouri*, Justia US Law, 4 May (1976) — the landmark case brought by the black women workers at a car manufacturing plant. This case is used to exemplify intersectional systemic racism and sexism and referred to by Kimberle Crenshaw, a leading scholar on intersectionality.

The Textile Clothing and Footwear Union of Australia (TCFUA) have advocated for consumers to be aware that 'distressed' jeans are wearing out the lungs of women workers across the world.

When the Hills Hoist Became the Wishing Tree (page 33)
Paphos is a coastal town, situated in the southwest of Cyprus and is renowned for the terebinth tree (the sacred tree that has roots reaching down to catacombs). Hanging from this tree's branches are handkerchiefs, ribbons and other types of cloth. These have been tied there by local and diasporic Cypriots, making wishes to Saint Solomoni.

The Quadrangle of Dreams (page 35)
The motto for the University of Melbourne is *Postera crescam lauáe*, Latin. A literal meaning: *Later I shall grow by praise*, reinterpreted: *We shall grow in the esteem of future generations.*

Goddess Nike (page 39)
Goddess Nike is the goddess of victory and is the University of Melbourne's symbol. Both symbol and motto are on the University's crest.

The Colour Chase (page 41)
abeer is also known as *gulal*, and is the traditional name given to the coloured powders used for the Hindu rituals, in particular for the Holi festival.

The Daily Commute (page 59)
The direct connection between Anisa Zahidee (lawyer) and Hidayet Ceylan (poet) as depicted in the poem is fictional. Although each person is a friend to the author who references them out of deep respect and admiration for their work, wisdom and creative output.

The Guest (page 65)
'Philoxenia' is a word with deep Greek roots pertaining to the general psyche of the Mediterranean people's show of hospitality and welcome, particularly to foreigners who are always received as guests.

After Dinner (page 67)
In mid-March 2020, due to the worldwide pandemic of the coronavirus disease 2019 (COVID-19), Melbourne progressed to 'social distancing' measures. Over the course of eight months, strict restrictions and 'lockdown' were activated for Melbourne residents.

Acknowledgements

Thank you to the poets, poetry editors and readers providing their invaluable feedback for this collection: Susan Hawthorne, Jena Woodhouse, Helen Nickas, Denise O'Hagan, Alex Skovron, Tricia Bowen. A special thank you to berni m janssen for formally launching the collection and to Spinifex Press for their unwavering support and guidance.

This collection would not have been possible without the support of the former National Languages and Literacy Board, and the Cypriot and Greek communities of Melbourne and abroad. Also, the support of my dear family Joshua, Elias and Theo Koch, and my second mother, Janet Andres.

Making Lace was first published in *Notata Online Arts Journal*, Number 1, March 2009, with subsequent acknowledged publications in *Southern Sun, Aegean Light,* Poetry of Second-Generation Greek-Australians, Edited N. N. Trakakis, 2011; *Mediterranean Poetry*, online journal, 11 November 2009 and partially referenced in Costi's essay: Reinventing the Ancient Across Four Cultures, One Ocean, *Cordite Poetry Review*, February 2013.

Somewhere Overseas an earlier version published in *Dinted Halos,* Hit&Miss Publications, 2003 and *The Other Side,* Issue 4, 2003.

The Weed Eaters and **The Good Citizens of Melbourne** published in *Mascara Literary Review,* 'Class Fetish' Issue 24, 2019.

The Colour Chase, Incident in Aisle 5 and **When the Hills Hoist Became the Wishing Tree** published in *The Blue Nib Literary Magazine*, international section, online, Issue 39, 2019 (Ireland).

Diagnoses published in *Australian Poetry Journal*, Volume 9, Number 2, 2019.

Shanker Hotel, New Delhi, 1991 published in *Cordite Poetry Review,* 93, November 2019.

Night Shift Crescendo published in the *Australian Multilingual Writing Project*, 3rd issue, November 2019.

Kostaki's Harvest Woes selected for *Verity La – Spirit of Home*, annual poetry reading and art event at Manly Art Gallery and Museum, 10 November 2019, and published in *The Ekphrastic Review*, July 2020 (Canada).

When Coburg Lake Became a Kyrenia Wedding published in *Panoply* (Literary Zine, USA), Issue 14, January 2020.

Refugee Aerobics published in *Unusual Work*, print publication, Number 28, Collective Effort Press, Melbourne, 2020.

Kinaesthetic Grace published in *StylusLit*, Issue 7, February 2020.

The Summit of Choice, The Daily Commute and **Shelter** published in *Eureka Street*, Volume 30, Number 7, 14 April 2020.

Shelter published on Poetry on the Move, 'Well-Known Corners of the People' <poetryonthemove.net> July 2020.

The Daily Commute and **Knock Knock** published in *Our Inside Voices – Reflections on COVID-19*, edited by Caroline Gardam, Louise Martin-Chew, Edwina Shaw and Nathan Shepherdson, 2020, AndAlso Books, QLD, Australia.

Abduction published in *The Blue Nib Literary Magazine, An Astrail*, online, June 2020 (Ireland) and *Australian Poetry Anthology*, Volume 8, 2020.

The English Missionary and **When the Hills Hoist Became the Wishing Tree** published in *Rochford Street Review*, Issue 28, June 2020.

From Bondi to Kyrenia, Fatigue and **Calling** published in *The Blue Nib Literary Magazine*, print, featured poet section, Issue 42, July 2020 (Ireland).

Australia Visits Minnesota and **Regulation** published in *Messages from the Embers – from Devastation to Hope: Australian Bushfire Poetry Anthology*, edited by Julia Kaylock and Denise O'Hagan, 2020, Black Quill Press, NSW. Australia.

Funding from the City of Melbourne COVID-19 Arts Grants, April 2020, enabled three poems in this collection (**Making Lace, Kinaesthetic Grace** and **Shelter**) to be produced as video poems for the Greek-Australian Cultural League (GACL) *Connection* exhibition 2020 <http://gaclmelbourne.com/g/artists-portrait-angela-costi/> These three poems and video poems were published in *Rochford Street Review*, Issue 29, September–October 2020. *Anagnostis*, 2020, Greek and English language, republished the three poems and video poems.

Good Night published in *Writers Resist*, Issue 119, October 2020 (USA).

Shelter 2nd place (tied), Meniscus Poetry Award 2020, University of Canberra.

The Quadrangle of Dreams published in *Antipodes*, Issue 66, 2020, Greek-Australian Cultural League (GACL), Melbourne.

Arrival published in *Right Now – Human Rights in Australia*, December 2020.

Frontline, Heavy, How to Drape a Saree, Kostaki's Harvest Woes published in *Hecate*, Volume 45.1 and 2, 2019.

Knock Knock published in *Writing in a Woman's Voice*, 6 January 2021 (USA).

An essay, *Unfolding Layers of Labour: a Cross-Generational Account of Kinaesthetic Skills*, by Angela Costi, weaves in the poems **Making Lace** and **Kinaesthetic Grace**, *The Journal of the Working-Class Studies*, Volume 5, Issue 3, December 2020.

*If you would like to know more about
Spinifex Press, write to us for a free catalogue, visit our
website or email us for further information
on how to subscribe to our monthly newsletter.*

Spinifex Press
PO Box 105
Mission Beach QLD 4852
Australia

www.spinifexpress.com.au
women@spinifexpress.com.au